Courtesy of Craig Studio

Plaque at location of Shiverick Shipyard
Shiverick Road, Sesuit Neck, East Dennis

Courtesy of Minerva Crowell Wexler

Wild Hunter
(1854-1881)

Courtesy of George R. King

Webfoot
(1856-1886)

They Built Clipper Ships in Their Back Yard

BY ADMONT G. CLARK

CLARK IMPRINTS
ORLEANS, MASSACHUSETTS

COPYRIGHT 2001 BY ADMONT G. CLARK
First printing 1963
Second Printing 1993
Third printing 2001

Reprinted (with additions) from *The American Neptune*, XXII (October 1962).

PHOTOGRAPHY BY THE CRAIG STUDIO, EAST DENNIS, MASSACHUSETTS

COVER DRAWING BY DOROTHY H. ELLEN

PRINTED BY JACK VIALL & NANCY VIALL SHOEMAKER, WEST HARWICH, MASSACHUSETTS

DISTRIBUTION BY ON CAPE PUBLICATIONS, YARMOUTHPORT, MASSACHUSETTS

TABLE OF CONTENTS

Preface	9
Introduction	9
The Shivericks and Their Shipyard	10
The Ships and Their Masters	13
Revenue	13
Hippogriffe	14
Belle of the West	15
Kit Carson	21
Wild Hunter	22
Webfoot	24
Christopher Hall	25
Ellen Sears	25
The Great Days End	25
Appendix A—The *Hippogriffe* Question	27
Appendix B—The *Christopher Hall* Story	28
Bibliography	29
Index	32

LIST OF ILLUSTRATIONS

Belle of the West	Cover
Plaque Commemorating the Shiverick Shipyard	1
Painting of *Wild Hunter* (Chinese)	2
Painting of *Webfoot* (William York of Liverpool, 1861)	2
The Joshua Sears Family:	17

    Captain Joshua Sears
    Mrs. Minerva Sears
    Louisa Sears

Builders' Half-Hull Models: 18

    Revenue, Built in 1850
    Hippogriffe, Built in 1852
    Belle of the West, Built in 1853
    Kit Carson, Built in 1854

Captains Christopher Hall and Prince S. Crowell	19
Captain Thomas Franklin Hall	20

They Built Clipper Ships in Their Back Yard

PREFACE

EVER since I moved to Dennis ten years ago and first heard of the Shiverick clipper ships they have fascinated me. But as I looked around for information I found that there has been no attempt made to tell the whole story of the Shivericks, their ships, and the men who sailed them. Of the sources, Dr. Kittredge provided the most information in his *Shipmasters of Cape Cod,* but of necessity in the entire context of his subject he treated this aspect lightly. Other references are extremely sketchy.

Since Dr. Kittredge credits the Shivericks with being 'the men who saved the Cape from having nothing but small craft to its credit,' and to satisfy my own curiosity, I decided to bring together from the many sources the information still available after nearly a century and weave it into a connected narrative of this great period. Unfortunately I had to limit my subject, for as I dug deeper I unearthed more raw material than I ever dreamed existed: logs, letters, bills, receipts, official documents, etc. There is a book here.

For much of the flavor of this article—as well as for the documentation of the *Hippogriffe* incident—I am indebted to Mrs. Minerva Crowell Wexler of Melrose and East Dennis. Further unpublished material came from the Joshua Sears family of East Dennis, descendants of the clipper ship captains.

I hope that I have contributed somewhat to the definitive history of Cape Cod, whose men since the earliest days of our country have loomed tall among those who follow the sea.

INTRODUCTION

One definition of art involves excellence of execution. By this definition the building of ships—particularly sailing ships—is an art, which reached its peak with the glorious clipper ships of the mid-nineteenth century. In the brief period from 1845 to 1860 American ships set nearly every permanent sailing record as they stormed around the world. Rivalry was keen, and the public followed this year-round race as closely as they now do the World Series. One of these records is held by Captain Milton P. Hedge and his *Webfoot*,[1] a 'back-yard clipper'[2] of East Dennis on Cape Cod.

No two of these great ships were exactly alike, for their builders (men like the great McKay, the equally great but less well-known Pook, and others) constantly strove for greater perfection. Shipmasters, owners, and builders each added a share to the magical yet quite hard-headed amalgam that was the clipper ship.

Cape Codders went forth in droves to officer the full-rigged fliers. 'In the matter of men no similar area produced more deep-water masters of outstanding ability than Cape Cod,' says one authority.[3] 'But the men who saved the Cape from having nothing but small craft to its credit [in shipbuilding] were the Shivericks'[4] of East Dennis.

From 1850 to 1862 out of Sesuit Creek, which runs between Sesuit and Quivet Necks (on which the village of East Dennis is built) came five medium and three extreme clippers, owned, built, and sailed by East Dennis men—a fleet of which the greatest merchant houses of the day, firms such as Glidden & Williams of Boston or Howland & Aspinwall of New York, could well be envious.

THE SHIVERICKS AND THEIR SHIPYARD

When Asa Shiverick, Senior, descended from Falmouth's first minister, the Reverend Samuel Shiverick,[5] moved down the Cape from Falmouth to East Dennis, the War of 1812 was in progress. Having learned the fundamentals of shipbuilding from Jeremiah Crowell in Dennis,[6] he bought land along Sesuit Creek, set up his own small yard, and began turning out brigs, sloops, and schooners. In 1815 a schooner came off his ways; in 1816, the brig *Polly;* in 1821 he worked on the packet schooner *David Porter,* to be used for regular runs to Boston; and in 1829 he pro-

[1] Carl C. Cutler, *Greyhounds of the Sea*, pp. 350-351.
[2] My phrase.
[3] Cutler, p. 368.
[4] Henry C. Kittredge, *Cape Cod—Its People and their History*, p. 146.
[5] Frederick Freeman, *The History of Cape Cod*, II, 717.
[6] Simeon L. Deyo (ed.), *History of Barnstable County, Massachusetts*, p. 527.

duced the topsail schooner *Atlas,* thriftily stripping the wreck of *Atlantic* which had recently come ashore, laden with flour, almost on his doorstep.[7]

Asa did not devote all his time to his shipyard. He had built a substantial house close to the yard in 1820,[8] and his three sons were reared there. Asa Junior, born in 1816, learned his trade in Lot Wheelwright's yard in Boston and later in Maine. David, too, worked in the Boston yards, studying drafting and modelmaking after his long day's work. Paul learned his trade from his father.[9] But all three learned well, for from 1835 to 1838 they and their father built and launched five vessels; and while they were at it each son built his own house along the road, each with a back yard reaching down to the tidewater of Sesuit Creek.

Asa Junior had come home in 1837,[10] a fair twenty-one-year-old and full of big ideas for the future—bigger ideas than just turning out little coasters. But adequate facilities had to be provided, plans laid, and money made. The tempo of the yard increased. *Bride, Grafton, Watchman,* and *Searsville,* to mention some, took the waters of Sesuit Creek (on a high-course tide).[11] They were good little vessels, these fishing schooners and coastwise packets.

Take *Bride,* for instance. In the 'awful October gale'[12] of 1841, which made widows and orphans up and down Cape Cod, with nine East Dennis men aboard she was caught and came ashore, pounded her masts out, and rolled over. All were lost. That day eleven others from the village vanished at sea, and of the lot twelve were Howeses, three were Crowells, and two were Searses[13]—all names flourishing in East Dennis today. And there lay *Bride,* seemingly a total loss. But the Shivericks refloated her and rerigged her, and off she sailed, as good as new.[14]

The boys—David and Paul and Asa Junior—had been out in the world. They had seen what was going on in the world-wide commerce of their country; they had helped to build the big and bigger ships that scudded out to China and the East Indies. They had seen hulls improve constantly in search of more speed.

So while they built boats in their back yards they dreamed and they schemed. They knew of *Ann McKim,* often called the first clipper, with

[7] *Idem.*
[8] *Idem.*
[9] Kittredge, *Cape Cod,* p. 148.
[10] Kittredge, *Cape Cod,* p. 138.
[11] Deyo, p. 527.
[12] Freeman, II, 713-714.
[13] Charles F. Swift, *History of Old Yarmouth,* pp. 255-256.
[14] Kittredge, *Cape Cod,* p. 139.

her finer bow, her deep after-drag, her pile of canvas. So had their neighbor across the creek on Quivet Neck, Captain Christopher Hall, who had amassed a competence as a shipmaster and now was operating his own fleet.[15]

Old Asa had retired and moved back to Falmouth, but his sons were eager to go on. The first step was to move the yard—lock, stock, adze, and maul—a half mile closer to the bay, in the lee of Sesuit Neck but close enough to deep water so that launching the big ships they planned would be much easier.[16] They placed their ways at an angle to the creek (just down the bank from the present commemorative stone) so that the thousand-tonners they would build could most easily take the water.

Today East Dennis is a quiet little village, living somewhat withdrawn from the passing world. But a hundred years ago the Shivericks made it a bustling, noisy place. Captain Thomas Franklin Hall, one of the very last of the clipper ship officers, and son of Captain Christopher Hall, thirty-five years ago recalled the scene vividly:

> I can well remember when the atmosphere of Quivet village (unlike today) reverberated to the music of mechanics' hammers and axes. . . .
> That harbor was the home port of a fleet of more than a score of vessels. Some of them, in summer time, were arriving and departing daily. . . . One schooner, the *David Porter*, as a packet, made constant trips back and forth to Boston, and one sloop, the *Star*, freighted salt, that was manufactured in this village. . . .
> Farther down the creek a wharf was constructed at the same time as the shipyard . . . on the east side of the creek, extending from the 'Island' creek bridge to the end of the present stone jetties. Adjoining the wharf were two large general stores, the only stores in Quivet village. . . .
> A steaming plant at the shipyard, for preparing timbers for bending, was located south of the road below the bluff. . . . The main shops were located north of the road. They consisted of a blacksmith shop, in charge of Heman Sears; an inboard joiner shop, in charge of James A. Smalley; a general carpenter shop operated by power, and a calkers' shop located at the foot of the hill below the other shops. Most of the workmen crossed the meadows to their homes on Quivet Neck over a foot bridge.[17]

The Shivericks and their neighbors were to build the ships; Captains Christopher Hall, Prince S. Crowell, and Levi Howes were to be the leading financiers (although most of the village owned shares);[18] and almost without exception the officers and future officers—masters, mates, and 'ship's cousins' or boys—were East Dennis men. Almost the only

---

[15] Henry C. Kittredge, *Shipmasters of Cape Cod*, p. 206.
[16] Thomas F. Hall, *The Significance of the Monument*.
[17] Hall.
[18] Kittredge, *Shipmasters*, p. 239.

elements of the entire enterprise that did not come from within a half mile of the Shivericks' back yards were the materials for the ships, which were delivered by water, principally from Maine, where Paul Shiverick chose with utmost care the oak and pine going into those massive hulls.[19]

The China trade was booming; *Sea Witch* staggered into New York under bare poles, 74 days from Canton, setting the permanent record.[20] The Liverpool packet lines were whittling away at time, and Europe was momentarily at peace. To the men of East Dennis, now was the time to make their fortunes.

Then, on 19 September 1848, the Washington *Union* announced the electric news of gold in California:

> We noticed in our last the arrival of Mr. Edward Fitzgerald Beale . . . who has performed the most rapid journey that has ever been known from the Pacific to Washington. . . .
>
> But the most extraordinary intelligence which Mr. Beale brings is about the real EL DORADO, the gold region in California. His accounts of the extraordinary richness of the gold surface, and the excitement it has produced . . . are confirmed by letters from Commodore Jones. . . .
>
> The danger in California is from want of food. . . . Would not some of our merchants find it profitable speculation to send cargoes of biscuit, flour, etc., round to the Pacific Coast?[21]

They would indeed, especially when it was found that even an expensive clipper, heavily manned as she had to be, more than paid for herself in one trip! East Dennis went to work.

The Ships and Their Masters

East Dennis went to work.

The little *Revenue,* medium clipper of only 546 tons, took the water in 1850 after considerable heaving and cussing by the able-bodied men from several towns, for she had broken down her ways at the first attempt.[22] Jury-rigged, she beat her way under reefs against a strong northwest gale to Boston, where she was sparred and rigged for sea.[23] Never a world-beater (perhaps she was too small), she nevertheless was a consistent earner, knowing all the oceans of the world, first under Captain Seth Crowell and then under Captain David Seabury Sears, both East Dennis

---

[19] Mary Shiverick Fishler, personal interview, 22 August 1960.
[20] Cutler, p. 137.
[21] Cutler, p. 132, quoting the Washington *Union,* 19 September 1848.
[22] Hall.
[23] *Idem.*

men. Twelve years old, tired and worn, she still fetched an offer of $20,000 in Genoa[24]—not enough for David Seabury, who sailed her home.[25]

Ultimately *Revenue* was sold in New York. Mr. Seleck Sears of East Dennis, grandson of Captain David Seabury Sears, recalls that his father, Ezra Sears, was destined for promotion to master of *Revenue* on her next trip and was bitterly disappointed at the sale.[26]

In 1852 *Hippogriffe*, 678 tons, 156 feet long, with a beam of 31 feet, was afloat.[27] These launchings were deft, dangerous affairs. Captain Hall describes them thus:

> The launchings always occurred during the high course tides in the early spring or fall. Even then there was not a great surplus of water, only enough to really float the larger ships for about one-half to three-quarters of an hour at each tide.
>
> Launching such large vessels into such a small stream was, therefore, at that time, and would be at this time, considered by the inexperienced a venturesome, daring undertaking....[28]

The captains of the ships were appointed sometimes before the keels were laid, and they assumed command as soon as the ship hit the water. Accordingly Captain Anthony Howes of East Dennis was in command of *Hippogriffe* on her trip to Boston for rigging, including the new Forbes's double topsails; in the following years he took her everywhere: maiden voyage to San Francisco and back, to Callao, to Calcutta, and back *via* the Cape of Good Hope to Boston.[29]

Consistently good passages were reported, but *Hippogriffe*'s main claim to fame is the finding of an uncharted rock in the Java Sea in 1858, with Captain Anthony Howes in command.[30] By consummate seamanship he got her off and brought her safe into Hong Kong, only to find that a large piece of the rock (probably coral) had broken off and neatly filled the hole that it had made in the bow. Hippogriffe Rock is on the charts today.[31]

After scarfing in new planking, Captain Howes set sail for London and ran into the worst storm of his career. Jib boom and foremast went over the side. The mainmast was sprung; the hull was badly strained. Un-

---

[24] Martin & Cavagna, unpublished letter to Captain Sears, 23 August 1862.
[25] *Log of Ship Revenue*, 1861-1862.
[26] Seleck M. Sears, unpublished letter to the author, 28 November 1960.
[27] Cutler, p. 421.
[28] Hall.
[29] Octavius T. Howe and Frederick C. Matthews, *American Clipper Ships, 1833-1858*, I, 266.
[30] See Appendix A for documentation.
[31] Kittredge, *Shipmasters*, pp. 244-245.

daunted, the crew went to work, fished the mainmast with spars and chain, rigged her as best they could, and limped into London, glad to be there at all.[32]

Aboard as first mate on that eventful trip was Daniel Willis Howes, another East Dennis man, who rose to become a shipmaster himself. On another occasion aboard *Hippogriffe,* with the captain sick, he quelled a mutiny by holding a redhot poker to the touchhole of the ship's cannon.[33]

On *Hippogriffe* went for another five years, until in 1863, with the Civil War raging and *Alabama* hunting Yankee ships across the world, Captain John H. Addy, Captain Prince S. Crowell's son-in-law, used his best judgment and sold her in Calcutta to the British, getting 70,000 rupees for her.[34]—more than her original cost.[35] This, to Captain Addy's mind, was a pretty good price, since at the same time *India* of Boston, 350 tons larger and five years younger, sold for only 90,000 rupees on the same terms.[36]

With their first two ships successful, the Shivericks aimed high. They prevailed on the great Samuel Hartt Pook of Boston to design *Belle of the West.* Pook was the young marvel of the era, second only to Donald Mc-Kay, acknowledged king of clipper ship designers. In 1846, when only twenty years old, he had designed the first large ocean-going steam tug, twin-screwed, iron-hulled, of 300 tons.[37] Naturally, he turned his talents to clippers and through ship after ship refined his ideas until a list of his designs reads like an *Almanach de Gotha* of sail. Captain Thomas Franklin Hall calls him 'the Praxiteles of his time.'[38]

There were *Red Jacket,* holder of the all-time record of thirteen days and one hour, dock to dock, from New York to Liverpool;[39] *Surprise,* in 1850 making her maiden voyage to San Francisco in the then record time of ninety-six days and fifteen hours, earning $78,000 freight on the voyage, and on the rest of her circumnavigation paying for her cost and expenses and netting her owners almost $50,000;[40] *Gamecock; Northern Light; Herald of the Morning; Telegraph; Fearless;* and *Challenger,* to mention some.[41]

[32] Kittredge, *Shipmasters,* pp. 244-245.
[33] *Idem.* But Daniel Willis had a reputation for telling tall stories; hence this one is fairly suspect.
[34] Howe and Matthews, p. 276.
[35] Kittredge, *Shipmasters,* p. 245.
[36] John H. Addy, unpublished letter to Prince S. Crowell, 22 December 1863.
[37] Cutler, p. 119.
[38] Hall.
[39] Cutler, p. 456, quoting New York *Herald,* 11 February 1854.
[40] Howe and Matthews, p. 461.
[41] Arthur H. Clark, *The Clipper Ship Era,* p. 271.

Pook's *Belle of the West* was the pride of the Shiverick fleet. Launched in 1853, just under 1,000 tons, 167 feet long,[42] she excited even blasé Boston, so used to nautical beauty.'The small fore-rake of her stem, with a lively sheer of 27 inches, and but slight flare of bows, gave her a most saucy and coquettish appearance,' says one source.[43] With her figurehead of a woman in flowing white, fringed with gold, she was called the handsomest ship to appear in San Francisco, and a newspaper said, 'Whatever bright-eyed little flirt she is named after, need not be ashamed of her appearance.'[44]

But Captain Thomas Franklin Hall, who knew her intimately, goes even further. Having grown up in her, he says:

> She was in my opinion the finest specimen of naval architecture ever seen.... She at last became my sweetheart, my idol, ... a graven image before which, for years, I daily bowed and worshipped, and although she has been lying in her grave at the bottom of the sea in the Bay of Bengal for sixty years, I would delight, if it were possible, to erect a marble shaft over the spot where her sacred bones are resting.[45]

Such a love as this, of a man for a ship, is by no means rare—and especially so in this period of the greatest beauty that sailors had ever seen.

More heavily sparred even than McKay's great *Flying Cloud*, which was 63 feet longer and had almost twice her tonnage,[46] *Belle* put to sea with Captain William Frederick Howes in command, once his leg, broken at her launching, had mended.[47] A skillful, conservative navigator, Captain Howes never 'drove' *Belle*. For that reason she is not a record holder, but 'many authorities state that she was never outsailed at sea.'[48] In the six years under Captain Howes she made two runs to San Francisco, the rest of the time operating with the regularity of a steamer in the East Indian trade.[49]

Taking over command from his brother, Captain Allison Howes continued the same steady work. In 1863 he chanced to meet a *third* brother, Captain Levi Howes, in Calcutta. Master of *Starlight*, 200 tons larger than *Belle*, Captain Levi challenged Captain Allison to a race home to Boston. *Starlight* left twelve hours ahead of *Belle;* they sighted each other three times during the voyage; and *Starlight* came into Boston twelve hours ahead of *Belle*[50]—a 17,000-mile dead heat.

[42] Cutler, p. 271.
[43] Howe and Matthews, p. 37.
[44] Ibid., p. 38.
[45] Hall.
[46] Howe and Matthews, I, 38.
[47] Hall.
[48] Howe and Matthews, ibid.
[49] Kittredge, *Shipmasters*, p. 183.
[50] Howe and Matthews, II, 629.

Captain Joshua Sears

Mrs. Minerva Sears

Louisa Sears

The Joshua Sears Family (Courtesy of Minerva Crowell Wexler)
On the maiden voyage of *Wild Hunter* (see page 22) Mrs. Sears and little Louisa accompanied Captain Sears, and Louisa rode her pony about the decks for exercise

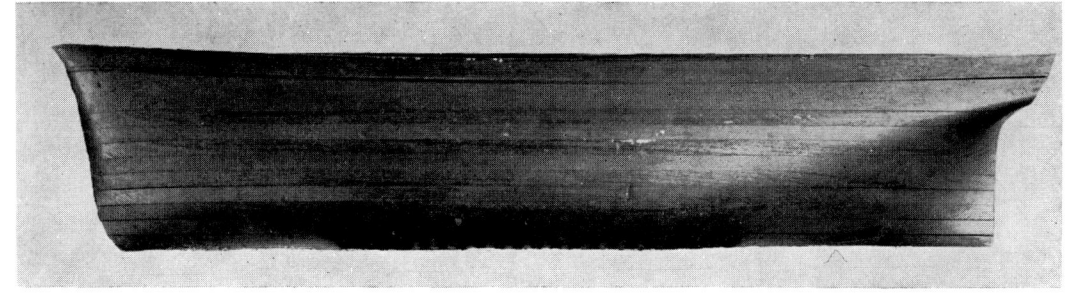

Revenue, built 1850   *Courtesy of Thomas Clark*

Hippogriffe, built 1852   *Courtesy of Thomas Clark*

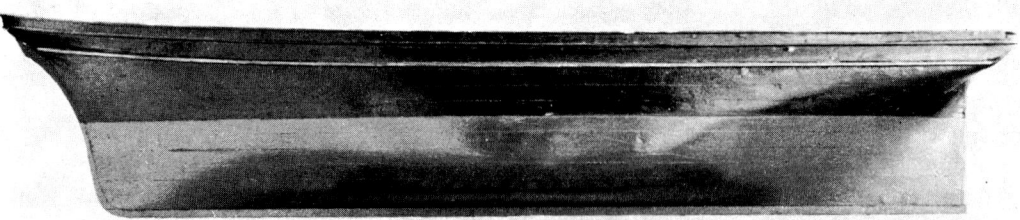

Belle of the West, built 1853   *Courtesy of Thomas Clark*

Kit Carson, built 1854   *Courtesy of Minerva C. Wexler*

A hull design begins with a builder's half-hull model, like these representing the first four Shiverick ships. The actual lines are taken off the model and expanded to full size. Note the hollow bows and extreme deadrise of *Belle*. *Kit Carson* keeps the hollow bow but has a flatter bottom

Courtesy of Minerva C. Wexler

Captain Prince F. Crowell

Courtesy of Gertrude Crowell

Captain Christopher Hall
(as a young man)

Courtesy of Gertrude Crowell

Courtesy of George R. King

Captain Thomas Franklin Hall, who was responsible for the commemorative plaque at the site of the Shiverick shipyard. The photograph on the right was probably taken about the time he and Heman Kelly ran away to the gold fields from *Wild Hunter*

Sold in 1864 to Mowjee Huny Doss of Calcutta and renamed *Fiery Cross*, she foundered in 1868 en route from Calcutta to Muscat with a cargo of rice.[51]

In 1854, *Kit Carson*, 1,016 tons, was launched, with Captain Seth Crowell of East Dennis as first master.[52] After a while Captain Prince S. Crowell, her owner, whose habit of trusting his captains' judgment was the talk of the merchant world, decided he'd try a different captain. Now, John Dillingham of Brewster was a fine seaman and a prolific letter writer, but he was no businessman.[53] In replying to a lyric description of the beauties of Puget Sound, Captain Crowell said:

> To go to Calcutta, one of the most expensive ports in the world, and take a cargo from there in the height of the monsoons at a rate equal to $8.50 a ton . . . exceeds by far all the miscalculations I ever heard of since I ever had anything to do with any ships.[54]

Captain Crowell trusted his men—but he had no patience with bad judgment.

Dillingham did not last long after that and was relieved in Liverpool by Captain Josiah Gorham of Yarmouth, who in turn was soon relieved by Captain Anthony Howes, former master of *Hippogriffe*.[55] Then came Captain Prince F. Crowell, son of owner Prince S. Crowell. His log of three years shows the following itinerary: Boston to San Francisco, to Callao, to Falmouth (England), to New York, to Montevideo, to Moulmein, and back to New York.[56]

But *Kit Carson*'s end was in sight. Having evaded Confederate cruisers all through the Civil War, she sailed into the River Plate, to find herself caught in the savage little War of the Triple Alliance (1865-1870), was commandeered, and ended her days as a block ship, sunk off Rio de Janeiro.[57]

As our Cape Cod clippers were beating about the world, the pendulum of world trade, which had started upward a full decade before, slowed in 1853 and started back down.[58] The California Gold Rush, with its $78,000 freights, had simmered down; the Australian Gold Rush of 1851,

---

[51] Ibid., I, 39.
[52] Cutler, p. 442.
[53] Kittredge, *Shipmasters*, p. 240.
[54] Prince S. Crowell, unpublished letter to John Dillingham, 17 March 1858.
[55] Kittredge, *Shipmasters*, p. 243.
[56] *Log of Ship Kit Carson*, 1863-1865.
[57] Hall.
[58] Cutler, pp. 280 ff.

which had attracted almost the same frenzied attention, was past; and the biggest single route left was the British tea trade, which American clippers had largely taken over from the British.[59] William John, the British writer, describes the situation thus:

> This new competition proved for a time most disastrous to English shipping, which was soon driven out of favor by the . . . famed speed of the American ships . . . and draughtsmen were sent from the Admiralty to take off the lines of two of the most famous—the *Challenge* and the *Oriental*—when they were in Messrs. Green's drydock.[60]

But East Dennis still saw a future in clippers—surprisingly in view of their higher initial cost, smaller capacity, and more expensive operation. But gradually as designers, led by Pook, realized that by eliminating the extreme dead rise (wedge shape of the bottom) they could greatly increase hull capacity at no sacrifice in speed, ships became fuller-bodied, almost flat at the keel. And they continued to set new records.[61] In 1854 *Red Jacket,* ship without extreme dead rise, made her famous run to Liverpool, during which she covered 413 miles in twenty-four hours,[62] an average for the day of 17.2 knots.

As the year of 1854 came to a close, the Shivericks and their neighbors erected the scaffolding and began framing and planking *Wild Hunter*. Down she came in 1855, the biggest yet at 1,081 tons, drawing 22½ feet.[63] She was given to Captain Joshua Sears, the only one of the East Dennis skippers who was a real driver.[64]

Earlier, as master of 'the old, square-bowed *Burmah*,' as he called her, he had worn her out racing against clippers to the Indies, often beating them. Later he had driven *Orissa* equally as hard in five round voyages to Calcutta.[65] *Orissa* was so heavily sparred that sailors called her 'Old Arms and Legs'; she ended her days on Cape Cod, driven ashore, sheathed in ice in January 1857. Local tradition has it that her deckhouse became one of the rooms of the Richard Kimball house in Orleans.[66]

Now *Wild Hunter* was his, and aboard as 'ship's cousin,' fifteen years old, was Thomas Franklin Hall, who recalls:

> Joshua Sears was as accomplished a sailor . . . as sailed the seas in those days. The

---

[59] Clark, p. 196.
[60] William John, 'American Clipper Ships,' *Naval Science*, II (1873), 265.
[61] Cutler, pp. 163-166, *passim*.
[62] Samuel E. Morison, *The Maritime History of Massachusetts*, p. 362.
[63] Cutler, p. 443.
[64] Howe and Matthews, II, 703.
[65] Kittredge, *Shipmasters*, pp. 157-158.
[66] Kittredge, *Mooncussers of Cape Cod*, pp. 102-103.

Wild Hunter in every port was a show, so complete in every respect was she kept. . . . Even a capstan bar could only be laid on deck pointing fore and aft.[67]

On her second trip to California Thomas Franklin and another boy, Heman Kelly, ran away to the gold fields. As Captain Joshua reported, 'It is the custom here for everybody to leave their ships, and they don't want to be behind the times.[68]

This particular Cape Cod skipper was not only a driver; he was far from the usual taciturn reporter of bare facts in his logs. Sailing for Singapore in ballast (no cargoes worth the taking) he records that he had a crew of 'two half-way sailors, white; eight boys; one shoemaker; four Manila men; three Malays and three Kanakas'[69]—twenty-one men to handle that tremendous spread of canvas.

Captain Joshua was not a patient man, either. He drove whenever he could, and when bedevilled by little or no wind he let off steam in his log:

Saturday, September 5. That heavy swell keeps running from the West. Patience, Patience,—Put your trust in God. Distance run 66 miles.
Sunday, September 6. . . . Slow getting along—Thy ways, O Lord, are inscrutable [*sic*].[70]

Driving, impatient, talkative—and seasick most of the time[71]—Captain Joshua is one of the most colorful of the clipper masters. A shrewd, hard bargainer, he conducted business on his own judgment for four years, receiving a salary of $200 a month. He was disgusted with his lack of success at finding cargoes that just were not there; for in 1857 a world-wide financial depression occurred, the results of which were felt until the Civil War.[72] He writes:

Oh for a cot in some vast wilderness where I shall never see a ship again. If ever one poor fellow was tired of anything, it is I, Josh Sears, that is sick and tired of going to sea.[73]

He retired to East Dennis, but *Wild Hunter* sailed on, first under Captain Baldry and then under Captain Thomas Prince Howes.[74] Finally in 1873 she was rerigged as a bark and sold.[75] Our last sight of her is a notice in the Boston *Transcript*, twenty-seven years after launching:

---

[67] Kittredge, *Shipmasters*, p. 206.
[68] Ibid., p. 207.
[69] *Log of Ship Wild Hunter*, 1857-1860.
[70] Ibid.
[71] Minerva Crowell Wexler, personal interview, 31 October 1960.
[72] Kittredge, *Shipmasters*, pp. 209-220, *passim*.
[73] *Log of Ship Wild Hunter*, ibid.
[74] Howe and Matthews, II, 704.
[75] Ibid., 705.

Fishing schooner *Colorado* of Gloucester has arrived at Halifax with crew of barque *Wild Hunter* from Boston to Revel, Russia, with cotton abandoned ninety miles off Halifax harbor, burning.[76]

With a sharp eye on developments in the field of design, the Shivericks next laid down *Webfoot,* classified as a medium clipper—fine, sharp, fast, but cleverly designed to carry large cargoes. She was the fastest of the Quivet fleet, for Captain Milton P. Hedge, who had her for the eight years she sailed American, drove her to one record (Calcutta to New York in eighty-five days in 1859) and to the second-fastest San Francisco-to-Liverpool passage (115 days in 1861).[77]

With her 1,091 tons register, she carried 2,160 weight and measurement tons to San Francisco on a voyage of 159 days[78]—a time which so disgusted Captain Hedge that he wrote a strong letter home to his owner, Captain Crowell. The reply is again typical of the man:

If you got in a bad scrape it's no use feeling so thundering bad, as that does not mend the matter; but keep a stiff upper lip. In regard to your proceedings, we are satisfied.[79]

The letter had the desired effect, for soon thereafter Captain Hedge hung up his record. During the Civil War he was busy in the Pacific guano trade, with side trips to Australia. In the spring of 1864, after grounding off Dunkirk, he decided to sell *Webfoot* to the British for £2,882, rather than pay twice that for repairs.[80]

Webfoot still had many good years in her. Rerigged as a bark, she traded about the world until 1886, when, a superannuated thirty-year-old, she sailed out of Puget Sound for Callao, loaded with lumber, and was abandoned, burning.[81]

As the depression of 1857 hit the world, Captain Christopher Hall, the man who had largely financed the back yard clippers, died. He would be sorely missed, for a more genial, generous shipowner there was not.[82] He selected his captains with care and then gave them the utmost freedom of judgment. Take the case of Captain Levi Howes, who, back in 1843, figured he had made enough money to retire. In New Orleans he met Captain Prince S. Crowell (still at that time sailing for Captain Hall); the

[76] Katharine Crosby, *Blue Water Men,* p. 123.
[77] Howe and Matthews, II, 685.
[78] Cutler, p. 515.
[79] Prince S. Crowell, unpublished letter to Captain Hedge, 15 May 1858.
[80] Howe and Matthews, II, 685.
[81] Ibid., 686.
[82] Kittredge, *Shipmasters,* p. 239.

two of them calmly swapped ships so that Captain Levi could get home faster. Captain Crowell wrote:

I suppose that you have been informed by L. Howes that he is coming home to Portsmouth in *Autoleon* . . . and that I am to take the *Ellen Brooks*.[83]

This loose state of affairs would have shocked almost any shipowner in the country—except another East Dennis man like Captain Crowell, who later was famous for giving the same latitude to his shipmasters. To the blue-water men of the village it made sense to rely on the judgment of the very men whom they had chosen to command.[84]

Captain Hall had always made it a habit to spread the prosperity brought by the ships among his friends and neighbors; most of the village owned at least some shares.[85] Thus by general consensus the ship then building was named for him. *Christopher Hall*, 648 tons (almost as small as *Revenue*), had an active ten-year career, first under Captain Joshua Freeman and then under Captain John H. Addy (previously of *Hippogriffe*), visiting such ports as Valparaiso, Calcutta, Rotterdam, Akyab, Hong Kong, Howland's Island (for guano), and many others before her complete loss on 19 January 1867, on an uncharted rock off Apia, in the Navigator Islands (now Western Samoa). All hands (including Mrs. Addy) escaped.[86] In a letter to his father-in-law Captain Addy complains about the high cost of passage to England—'60 pounds a piece.'[87]

In 1862 the last of the series, *Ellen Sears,* was built by the Shivericks for their own account and sold even before launching for more than the $70,000 she had cost them.[88] Captain Joseph Henry Sears of Brewster, her owner and a colorful character in his own right, had her named for his sister.[89] *Ellen's* career was the shortest, for in 1867, under Captain J. F. Bartlett of Brewster, she disappeared somewhere between San Francisco and Liverpool—another in the long tale of tragedies at sea.[90]

The Great Days End

The Civil War was raging. East Dennis played a strong part in men and ships; with the village stripped of men, there was little point in con-

---

[83] Kittredge, *Shipmasters*, p. 152.
[84] *Idem.*
[85] Ibid., p. 239.
[86] *Vide* appendix B.
[87] John H. Addy, unpublished letter to Prince S. Crowell, 1 March 1867.
[88] Katharine Crosby, *Blue Water Men and Other Cape Codders*, p. 176.
[89] Dean S. Sears, personal interview, 1 December 1960.
[90] J. Henry Sears, *Brewster Ship Masters*, p. v.

tinuing the yard. It was closed and dismantled. Half of the main workshop traveled across the creek to become a barn. The other half moved up the road; and the oakum shop moved to Punkhorn Hollow and became a house.[91] The tools—adzes, wedges, and mauls—fetched up in barns all over town and are there today.

The Shivericks themselves dispersed. Paul went south to get out phosphate rock for the fertilizer factory in Woods Hole of which Asa, Junior, became manager in 1862. Then he went west to work for Captain Thomas Franklin Hall, who in 1866 had trekked to Omaha and there set up the territory's first machine shop and foundry.[92]

Captain Prince S. Crowell turned to his other pursuits such as his bank, the Cape Cod and Old Colony Railroads, and the Pacific Guano Company, a fertilizer factory which he had organized in 1859 with the help of Boston and New York capital (the famous Hetty Green is said to have held an interest in it). It is a safe assumption that the factory was established largely to provide his ships (and others) with a valuable cargo—guano from Howland's Island in the Pacific and Great Swan Island in the Caribbean—during the lean days of world shipping. The factory also made chemical fertilizers and sulphuric acid.[93]

Prince Crowell was a considerable figure in the financial world, and even more importantly in the antislavery movement. For many years his home was a well-known station on the Underground Railroad.[94] Parker Pillsbury, the ardent reformer, on 11 December 1881, gave an address *in memoriam* of Captain Crowell and had this to say about him:

> While in the vigor of his manhood he left the sea, but only for more active service on the shore. . . . While still having extensive interests in commerce, foreign and domestic, he entered largely into railroad construction, commencing in his own neighborhood, here by the Atlantic, though extending across the continent to the Pacific. But not only did he make the soil more valuable by multiplying the means of transportation, . . . but by invention and improving of *fertilizers* he has shown how even the lands of Cape Cod may be made to bloom like Eden.
> . . . But as Bank President and Director, as Director in the Cape Cod and Old Colony Railroads, as one of the original corporators and largest owners in the Pacific Guano Company, his record . . . proves him to have possessed both ability and integrity of the highest order, even in these degenerate times.[95]

The East Dennis clippers were extremely successful ships, although the career of *Ellen Sears* was all too brief. With the exception of *Webfoot*

---

[91] Mary Shiverick Fishler, personal letter of 12 October 1960.
[92] *Idem.*
[93] Dorothy G. Wayman, *Suckanesset*, pp. 43-44.
[94] Minerva Crowell Wexler, personal interview, 31 October 1960.
[95] Parker Pillsbury, *Address in Memoriam*, p. 10.

they made no records, but they made many profitable voyages and delivered their cargoes intact. Nobody ever accused a Cape Codder of being much but 'free, self-reliant, frugal, and indomitable,'[96] and the captains — the Howeses, the Crowells, the Halls, the Searses, East Dennis men all — although they were skillful seamen, preferred a comfortable profit in freight to a record-smashing try that would cost hard-won cash for repairs. As a group the ships were long-lived; some were ancients; but only one (*Christopher Hall*) was lost while East Dennis men owned and sailed them.

But the village still remembers dimly the great days. The Shiverick houses are still there on Sesuit Neck (one of them until this year occupied by a Shiverick). The captains' descendants still live in the captains' houses and cherish the few mementos that have survived time and living. On the surface East Dennis looks much the same as in the days of greatness, a hundred years ago, but the noisy bustle of the Shiverick shipyard has disappeared as completely as the ships built there.

Perhaps the last word on this magnificent village venture belongs rightly to Captain Thomas Franklin Hall, who participated in it; speaking of the commemorative stone and plaque marking the site of the yard (the only evidence we moderns are now able to see) Captain Hall said:

To understand clearly the high standard reached in developing those ships, it should be remembered that they were built during the years when the American Mercantile Marine was in the very zenith of its fame and glory. . . . When, therefore, it is realized that ships from the Shiverick yard were not only equal, but in some technical respects, superior to any in the American fleet, it is more than gratifying to local pride; . . .

It was a masterful undertaking . . . to establish such an enterprise in such a quiet spot, on the banks of such a small stream. Yet it is due entirely to the modesty and reticence of those giant intellects that this village is not renowned for the masterpieces it sent out. . . .

Those were great years; great events; great men.[97]

Appendix A

The *Hippogriffe* Question

The grounding of *Hippogriffe* in 1858 has been a source of considerable doubt. Just who was in command—and even just *where* it happened—as well as what type of shoal it was that she hit—have been given various answers over the years. Howe and Matthews, in *American Clipper Ships*, I, 266, the acknowledged authorities on the era, imply that David Seabury Sears was in command and state that the grounding was in the China Sea. There is a strong local tradition in favor of Sears as the culprit, rather than Anthony Howes.

[96] Deyo, p. 11.
[97] Hall.

Following Howe and Matthews, Atwood, Crosby, and most others ascribe the grounding to Sears. But Dr. Kittredge in *Shipmasters of Cape Cod* gives the captain as Anthony Howes and the location as the *Java* Sea. I asked Dr. Kittredge if, after twenty-five years, he could recall the source of his information; not surprisingly, he could not.

However, in going over the same ground I found it. In the possession of Mrs. Minerva Crowell Wexler are the originals of:

(1) the warrant for survey of *Hippogriffe* issued by Robert B. Campbell, U. S. Consul to the Port of London (and, oddly enough, unsigned although sealed);
(2) the three surveys made on the ship;
(3) the certificate of seaworthiness issued by the London Surveyor of Shipping upon completion of repairs.

In all cases Anthony Howes is named as master and the stranding is placed in the Java Sea.

As to the character of the shoal, Corbett (*Cape Cod's Way*, p. 237) states that according to the diary of the first mate (who was Daniel Willis Howes, the alleged queller of a mutiny aboard *Hippogriffe*) it was merely a sand bar and not a rock at all, thus denigrating the story of the hole in the bow neatly filled by a piece of rock (probably coral).

Primary evidence can be quite unreliable; such is the case here, for the British Admiralty's survey ship *Swallow* in 1866 located and charted the rock, described as follows in *The China Sea Directory* of 1867:

HIPPOGRIFFE SHOAL.—Mr. Wilds [commanding H. M. survey ship *Swallow* in 1866] also searched for the Hippogriffe Shoal, and found it in lat. 3° 33′ 36″ S., long. 106° 54′ 30″ E. It is a dangerous boulder rock, with only 3 feet over it at low water, of circular shape, and about 150 feet in diameter, having large branches of coral upon it. It was not seen until close to, and at the time it was examined there was not the slightest swell or ripple to indicate its position; the weather being fine and clear, and the wind light from the S.S.E. Regular soundings of 8 fathoms, sand and shell, were found around it, and the water in that depth was of a pale color.[98]

Historically, then, Captain Anthony Howes was in command; the incident occurred in the Java Sea; and it is quite likely that a piece of the coral around the rock broke off and filled the hole punched in the bow.

Appendix B

The *Christopher Hall* Story

Beyond the bare fact that the Shivericks built a ship named *Christopher Hall*, all authorities in print give no details whatever about her career—not even her tonnage. In an attempt to round out the Shiverick story, I therefore went to my best source of unpublished information, Mrs. Minerva Crowell Wexler, with my problem. She was able to give me considerable assistance, so that I now have a fair idea of her entire career and details of her untimely end off Apia.

[98] J. W. Reed and J. W. King, *The China Sea Directory*, pp. 100-101.

BUILT CLIPPER SHIPS IN BACK YARD

To avoid extending my bibliography with *minutiae*, I have not listed the following documents, which picture the ship's occupation fairly well from 1858 to her end:

    1858, 17 November—Receipt for coal, Boston to San Francisco
    1859, 15 June—Receipt for water, Valparaiso
    1860, 7 January—Consular receipt, Liverpool
    1861, 19 October—Consular receipt, Hong Kong
    1862, 20 November—letter from Addy to Crowell, Cardiff
    1862, 15 December—Receipt for water, Valparaiso
    1863, 22 December—Letter from Addy to Crowell, Calcutta
    1864, 11 October—Custom receipt, Cardiff
    1865, 18 April—Consular receipt, Akyab
    1865, December through March, 1866—Eleven letters from Addy to Crowell, New York
    1866, 24 July—Letter, Addy to Crowell, Hong Kong
    1866, 19 August—Letter, Addy to Crowell, Shanghai
    1866, 26 December—Letter, Addy to Crowell, Howland Island

It was on the voyage from Howland Island to Apia that the ship was lost, as evidenced by Captain Addy's Note of Protest, filed at Apia on 21 January 1867.

BIBLIOGRAPHY

Books and Pamphlets:
Atwood, Alfred Ray. *Sermon for Ship Sunday, July 24, 1932*. N.p., n.d.
Baker, Florence W. (ed.) *Yesterday's Tide*. Yarmouth Port, Mass.: The Register Press, 1941.
Bray, Mary Matthews. *A Sea Trip in Clipper Ship Days*. Boston: Richard G. Badger, 1920.
Brigham, Albert Perry. *Cape Cod and the Old Colony*. New York: G. P. Putnam's Sons, 1921.
Chatterton, E. Keble. *The Ship Under Sail*. Philadelphia: J. B. Lippincott and Company, 1909.
Clark, Arthur H. *The Clipper Ship Era*. New York: G. P. Putnam's Sons, 1911.
Corbett, Scott. *Cape Cod's Way*. New York: Thomas Y. Crowell Company, 1955.
Crosby, Katharine. *Blue Water Men and Other Cape Codders*. New York: The Macmillan Company, 1946.
Cutler, Carl C. *Greyhounds of the Sea:* The Story of the American Clipper Ship. New York: Halcyon House, 1930.
Deyo, Simeon L. (ed.) *History of Barnstable County, Massachusetts*. New York: H. W. Blake and Company, 1890.
Freeman, Frederick. *The History of Cape Cod:* The Annals of Barnstable County and of its Several Towns, Including the District of Mashpee, two volumes. Boston: Geo. C. Rand & Avery, 1858.
Hall, Thomas Franklin. *The Significance of the Monument and Tablet Recently Erected at the Shiverick Shipyard Site in East Dennis, Massachusetts*. Yarmouth *Register*, January 16 and January 23, 1926. (Later published as "Ship-Building in East Dennis." *Library of Cape Cod History and Genealogy, No. 11.* Yarmouthport, Mass.: C. W. Swift, n.d.)

Harris, Charles E. *Hyannis Sea Captains.* Yarmouth Port, Mass.: The Register Press, 1939.
Howe, Henry F. *Salt Rivers of the Massachusetts Shore.* New York: Rinehart and Company, 1951.
Howe, Octavius T., and Frederick C. Matthews, *American Clipper Ships, 1833-1858,* two volumes. Salem, Mass.: Marine Research Society, 1927.
Kittredge, Henry C. *Cape Cod—Its People and Their History.* Boston: Houghton Mifflin Company, 1930.
Kittredge, Henry C. *Mooncussers of Cape Cod.* Boston: Houghton Mifflin Company, 1937.
Kittredge, Henry C. *Shipmasters of Cape Cod.* Boston: Houghton Mifflin Company, 1935.
LaGrange, Helen. *Clipper Ships of America and Great Britain.* New York: G. P. Putnam's Sons, 1936.
Laing, Alexander. *Clipper Ship Men.* New York: Duell, Sloan and Pearce, 1944.
Morison, Samuel Eliot. *By Land and By Sea.* New York: Alfred A. Knopf, 1953.
Morison, Samuel Eliot. *The Maritime History of Massachusetts, 1783-1860.* Boston: Houghton Mifflin Company, 1921.
Pillsbury, Parker. *In Memoriam:* An Address in Memory of Capt. Prince S. Crowell, Who Died November 5, 1881: Delivered in Association Hall, East Dennis, Mass., on Monday, December 11, 1881. N.p., n.d.
Pratt, Enoch. *A Comprehensive History, Ecclesiastical and Civil, of Eastham, Wellfleet and Orleans.* Yarmouth, Mass.: W. S. Fisher and Co., 1844.
Rich, Shebnah, *Truro—Cape Cod; or Land Marks and Sea Marks.* Boston: D. Lothrop and Company, 1884.
Reed, J. W., and J. W. King. *The China Sea Directory:* Containing Directions for the Approaches to the China Sea and to Singapore, by the Straits of Sunda, Banka, Gaspa, Carimata, Rhio, Varella, Durian, and Singapore. London: Printed for The Hydrographic Office, Admiralty, 1867.
Sears, J. Henry. *Brewster Ship Masters.* Yarmouthport, Mass.: C. W. Swift, 1906.
Swift, Charles F. *Cape Cod, the Right Arm of Massachusetts.* Yarmouth, Mass.: The Register Publishing Company, 1897.
Swift, Charles F. *History of Old Yarmouth, 1639-1884.* Yarmouthport, Mass.: The Author, 1884.
Trayser, Donald G. (ed.) *Barnstable:* Three Centuries of a Cape Cod Town. Hyannis, Mass.: F. B. and F. P. Goss, 1939.
Wayman, Dorothy G. (Theodate Geoffrey). *Suckanessett:* Wherein May Be Read a History of Falmouth, Massachusetts. Falmouth, Mass.: The Falmouth Publishing Company, Inc., 1930.

Periodicals:
John, William. 'American Clipper Ships,' *Naval Science,* II (1873), 265.

Unpublished Works:
Addy, John H. Personal Letter to Prince S. Crowell. Calcutta, 22 December 1863.
Addy, John H. Note of Protest Regarding Loss of *Christopher Hall.* Apia, Navigator Islands, 21 January 1867.
Addy, John H. Personal Letter to Prince S. Crowell. Apia, Navigator Island, 1 March 1867.

Campbell, Robert B. Warrant for Survey of *Hippogriffe*. London, 22 February 1859.
Campbell, Robert B. Certificate of Good Repute. London, 28 April 1859.
Crowell, Prince S. Personal Letter to Milton P. Hedge. East Dennis, Mass., 15 May 1858.
Crowell, Prince S. Personal Letter to John Dillingham. East Dennis, Mass., 17 March 1858.
Fishler, Mary Shiverick. Personal Letter to the Author. Ridgewood, New Jersey, 12 October 1960.
Freeman, Joshua. Statement of General Average. New York, 1862.
Kit Carson. Log for Years 1863-1865.
Martin & Cavagna. Business Letter to David Seabury Sears. Marseilles, 23 August 1862.
Reeves, Peter John. Certificate of Seaworthiness for *Hippogriffe*. London, 20 April 1859.
Reeves, Peter John, and Frederick Burnham. Report of Survey of *Hippogriffe*. London, 23 February 1859.
Reeves, Peter John, and Frederick Burnham. Report of Survey of *Hippogriffe*. London, 10 March 1859.
Reeves, Peter John, Frederick Burnham, and Edmund Hammond. Report of Survey of *Hippogriffe*. London, 17 March 1859.
Revenue. Log for Years 1861-1862.
Sears, Seleck M. Personal Letter to the Author. St. Petersburg, Florida, 28 November 1960.
Wild Hunter. Log for Years 1857-1860.

Personal Interviews:

Fishler, Mary Shiverick. Personal Interview, 22 August 1960.
Sears, Dean S. Personal Interview, 29 November 1960.
Wexler, Minerva Crowell. Personal Interview, 31 October 1960.

Captain Admont G. Clark, USCGR, Retired, "swallowed the anchor" on Cape Cod shortly after World War II. For fourteen years, he taught at the Massachusetts Maritime Academy. An occasional author, he has published in Cosmopolitan, Yankee, The Rotarian, *among others. He was a founding member and first president in 1954 of the Cape Cod Museum of Natural History. In 1961, he joined the first faculty of the newly-opened Cape Cod Community College, from which he retired as a full professor in 1983. He is still teaching there part-time.*

INDEX

Addy, Captain John H., 15, 25, 29.
Ann McKim, clipper ship of Baltimore, 11.
Atlas, Shiverick schooner, 11.
Australian Gold Rush, 21.
Baldry, Captain, 23.
Belle of the West, Shiverick clipper ship, 15-21.
Bartlett, Captain J. F., of Brewster, 25.
Bride, Shiverick schooner, 11.
Burmah, ship, 22.
California Gold Rush, 13, 21.
Challenge, clipper ship, 22.
Challenger, clipper ship designed by Pook, 15.
Christopher Hall, Shiverick clipper ship, 25, 27, 28-29.
Crowell, Jeremiah, of Dennis, shipbuilder, 10.
Crowell, Captain Prince F., 21.
Crowell, Captain Prince S., 12, 15, 21, 24-25, 26.
Crowell, Captain Seth, 13, 21.
David Porter, Shiverick schooner, 10, 12.
Dillingham, Captain John, of Brewster, 21.
East Dennis, 10, 12, 13, 22, 25, 27.
Ellen Sears, Shiverick clipper ship, 25, 26.
Fearless, clipper ship designed by Pook, 15.
Flying Cloud, clipper ship designed by McKay, 16.
Gamecock, clipper ship designed by Pook, 15.
Gorham, Captain Josiah, of Yarmouth, 21.
Grafton, Shiverick schooner, 11.
Hall, Captain Christopher, 12, 24-25.
Hall, Captain Thomas Franklin, 12, 15, 16, 22-23, 26, 27.
Hedge, Captain Milton P., 10, 24.
Herald of the Morning, clipper ship designed by Pook, 15.
Hippogriffe, Shiverick clipper ship, 14, 15, 21, 25, 27-28.
Hippogriffe Rock or Shoal, 14, 28.
Howes, Captain Allison, 16.
Howes, Captain Anthony, 14, 21, 27-28.
Howes, Captain Daniel Willis, 15, 28.
Howes, Captain Levi, 12, 16, 24-25.
Howes, Captain Thomas Prince, 23.
Howes, Captain William Frederick, 16.
John, William, British writer, 22.
Kelly, Heman, 23.
Kit Carson, Shiverick clipper ship, 21.
Kittredge, Dr. Henry C., 9, 26.
Northern Light, clipper ship designed by Pook, 15.
Oriental, clipper ship, 22.
Orissa, ship, 'Old Arms and Legs,' 22.
Pacific Guano Company, 26.
Pillsbury, Parker, 26.
Polly, Shiverick brig, 10.
Pook, Samuel Hartt, naval architect, 15, 16, 22.
Punkhorn Hollow, 26.
Quivet Neck, 10, 12.
Quivet village, 12.
Red Jacket, clipper ship designed by Pook, 15, 22.
Revenue, Shiverick clipper ship, 13-15, 25.
Sea Witch, clipper ship, 13.
Sears, Captain Ezra, 14.
Sears, Captain Joseph Henry, of Brewster, 25.
Sears family, Joshua, 9.
Sears, Captain Joshua, 22-23.
Sears, Seleck, 14.
Searsville, Shiverick schooner, 11.
Sesuit Creek, 10-11.
Sesuit Neck, 10, 27.
Shiverick, Asa, Jr., 11, 26.
Shiverick, Asa, Sr., 10, 11, 12.
Shiverick, David, 11.
Shiverick, Paul, 11, 13, 26.
Shiverick, Reverend Samuel, 10.
Star, Shiverick sloop, 12.
Starlight, clipper ship, race with *Belle of the West*, 16.
Surprise, clipper ship designed by Pook, 15.
Telegraph, clipper ship designed by Pook, 15.
Transcript, Boston newspaper, 23-24.
Triple Alliance, War of the, 21.
Underground Railroad, 26.
Union, Washington newspaper, report of gold find, 13.
Watchman, Shiverick schooner, 11.
Webfoot, Shiverick clipper holding two records, 10, 24, 26.
Wild Hunter, Shiverick clipper, 22-24.
Wexler, Minerva Crowell, 9, 28.

Cover Stock is Recycled Paper